Letters to an Angel

(Part One of Xander's Memorial Website Posts)

For Xander
RIP
May 17, 1982 - August 14, 2004

Letters To An Angel
(Part One of Xander's Memorial Website Posts)

ISBN: 978-0-6151-5332-2
Posts written by each author credited
©2007

Letters to an Angel is part of a series of poetry and memorial books published post-mortem, on behalf of Xander's family. Special thanks to Xander's mother and grandmother, D and Wilma, for helping preserve the memory of Xander, and all of his amazing works.

Edited and Designed by Timothy Bowen

OTHER BOOKS AVAILABLE:

Never Forget Me
Love's Confusing Joy
Thinking of You

All available at : http://www.lulu.com/wilmabrecheen1

to post your thoughts or memorials to Xander please visit:
http://www.xandersmith.org/forum/

your memorials could end up in further editions of this work

I am in the flowers that bloom.
I am in a quiet room.
I am in the birds that sing.
I am in each lovely thing.

So do not stand by my grave and cry.
I am not there.
I did not die.

note from the editor:

I tried my best to keep each of these entries exactly how they were, spelling mistakes and all. I know Xander wouldn't have cared if someone didn't capitalize the "I" or forgot to put it before "E." I also tried my best to put a picture next to each person's entry of them with Xander, however it was impossible to do that with *every* entry. On the second page of this book is a website address where you can leave more letters to this angel, and if you think you'd like it to be published in a further volume, might I suggest including your own pictures with Xander, or whatever else you'd like to go in it.

Much love to everyone who's left a memorial, and I hope you all get a copy of this book to cherish forever along with your memories of Xander.

If I forgot to put an entry in, and you would like it put in the next book, email me directly at billybobgrammar@gmail.com and I'll gladly include you!!

NOW I CAN WEEP
by David Brecheen

These same hot tears burned
down my cheeks
As we watched the dawn rush
toward us
From across the misty lake.
We talked,
laughed,
and cried together.
We wept then for ourselves and
one another
But mostly for those we loved.
Because so few of them could
know.

You had so little left to learn
And as I watched the morning
light
rushing toward you--I felt the
chill
even before you told me.

There were some who knew,
before you left.
And others who would know
when you were gone.
Your Grandma knew--my sister.
All she could know with her
mind, and all the rest
she knew with her heart.

Long long ago--when you were
the great teacher
And I sat at your feet and listened
And I knew.

At least it felt that way, when we
shared our
knowledge, and tears, and
laughter.
And watched the light approach.

Now you are gone.
You left this world, and
Now you've left my reach
And I miss you.

You are gone.
That supersedes all theology
and speculation.
You'll not be back here again.
Not to live.
We will all miss you,
because you loved us all.

I received a book you wrote.
"Never Forget Me"
You've got to be kidding!
I couldn't forget you, Ever,
Even if you had never been born.

"Never Forget Me"
It told me you were gone,
Even from me, and for a while
I felt the burning on my cheeks,
And I was glad I could weep.

So long, Old Friend.
Save me a place in the stars.

David

Lisa Parks

Your picture was in the paper yesterday, and I just can't believe that you have been gone for a whole year now.

This is going to sound weird, but I had a dream about you a couple of months ago that really touched me. You see, I have this reoccurring nightmare where I'm on the Titanic and it's going down. Well, I was having this dream, and here you came, Xander--calm and cool out of the blue. The instant I saw you, I realized the ship around me was all a dream, but you were real. You started multiplying. I think there were at least three or four of you around me. I got the sense that you were everywhere, and you could talk to many different people at the same time. (There were other people around us that I didn't know, but you were holding perfectly good conversations with them all even as you were talking to me.) I hugged you and told you I loved you. We were able to communicate without moving our mouths. It was something like mind-speak, I guess. I got the sense that you knew everything and I could ask you anything. I had all sorts of questions to ask, but you told me you couldn't stay long. The last thing I remember is you holding a large blue bowl. After waking from this dream, I consulted a dream dictionary about the blue bowl. It meant something like "security or faith in heaven." Since having that dream, I have felt better. I've read on your message board that other people have had similar experiences, like Erin and her bird, and I think you are trying to tell us that you really are with us all.

It was really hard sitting in the auditorium at Les Miserables at JHS. I had been Fantine to your Javert, when we did Les Mis with the Youth Rep under Mark Landon Smith's direction. You were amazing as Javert! I remember that there was a line in the script where Javert was supposed to say "Damn you, Valjean!" Well, being the Youth Repertory, Mark Smith changed your line to "Darn you, Valjean!" During our final rehearsal, as you were waiting in the wings for your entrance, you whispered to all of us that you were going to change the line back! We all held our breaths as we watched you make your entrance on stage and yell that cuss word as loud as you could! I believe that was the last line of Act 1, and the minute the stage went dark, you scampered off like a squirrel, laughing in the way that only you could. Mark Smith was not so amused, but we all exploded in laughter. It is just one of those special Xander moments.

I think about you often. No one in my life has ever made me laugh as much as you did. You simply dazzled, and I will miss you forever. My life would not have been the same without you. I read your Memorial Page from time to time, and it never ceases to amaze how greatly you touched so many lives.

I love you,
Lisa

Bryen Miller

I know it has been a while since my last visit. I think about you often, almost everyday. I have had so many topics on my plate the past few months; I find my life is slowly coming out of chaos to a sense of calm. So calm that it scares me. However, in the midst of this calm, I realized, I didn't make it here in time for your birthday. Happy Birthday Xander.

I actually remembered it, however, I've been on a spiritual healing of sorts and in a way you have been there with me. I think I've had you in my thoughts everyday the past month or so. I must admit, I was in a dark hole 4-5 weeks ago, until I made a great friend who pulled me up and back into life. Is it any surprise that he reminds me of you in a few important ways? That's why you've occupied my thoughts so frequently.

After hanging out one weekend with my new friend, I realized how much I miss you and how just being in your presence made me feel. I came home and suddenly burst into tears, my emotions overloaded. You always gave off such a positive energy and never made me question myself or doubt myself. You simply had a way of making me feel relaxed to just be me. That's such a wonderful quality to have, especially on someone like me who tends to be hard on myself.

There where so many times when, for some reason or another, I just never was sure that I "fit in" with everyone - a fish out of water. But if you were there, you seemed to just erase those thoughts from my head. I have met very few, if just only a handful of people that give off such an inspiring positive radiance.

My friend doesn't let me get down and out and stay withdrawn, and you never did either. No matter how hard I would resist, you always got me to break out of my introverted shell and have a great time, especially when I needed it the most.

I know there were times, I probably wasn't the most fun to be around or the greatest company. You saw some of the rawness during a very hard breakup. I feel bad for that and wish I had come to the truths that I have today. I haven't been the person I want to be the past several years, but slowly I'm working on bringing out the better sides of me.

Xander you always brought out the best in me. I keep that in mind while I'm on this journey of self improvement. There are times when I wonder, what will I have to leave behind? How will anyone know I was here? Then I think of you, honest and truthfully. Xander you were only a part of my life for a few years, but you have left a profound effect on me that I will take with me always. You will always be a part of me. So, if I can do the same to someone else...well, what a profound legacy to leave and have passed on. Thank you for being a part of my life.

Love,
Bryen

Bryen Miller

As both a friend and former roommate, I am so grateful to have had Xander in my life. Compassion, respect and concern for others were of second nature to him. He had such a warm light in his spirit and incredible energy to his heart; you could just feel his enthusiasm for life influence you. Whenever I was feeling down or upset, he always just knew the right words to say to make me smile or laugh. Our late night conversations on life, love, religion, and all things in-between provided me with a new way of understanding myself and what life was really about. He always told me to be true to myself, my friends and my passion. Xander's passion for his music inspired and moved me. I always enjoyed sitting with him as he worked on the lyrics for a new song. One of my favorite songs he wrote helped me get through a very difficult time in my life. The song precisely captured my feelings and it was comforting to know he could understand exactly what I was feeling. It was entitled "Left Too Soon." I never would have ever imagined how symbolic that song would become for such a talented and gifted artist. Xander, may you live on through your music and poetry. You will always be deeply loved; you will always be deeply missed.

Nancy Nelson

Xander was so blessed with so many talents you couldn't write them all down. He will be missed by many. His memory will live on forever.

Brian Pickler

A sparkling gem and a wonderful talent who made an impression to everyone on Earth and will continue to do so in Heaven.

Much Love

Lee Jarrod Evans

Hi. Reading the messages on this page I am truly elated. Xander is a wonderful person that has obviously touched many people and who's infinite spirit will continue to bring joy. I believe this is something Xander understood, ENERGY IS INFINITE. I enjoyed all the times we had man, your understanding of esoteric concepts and your ability to communicate them has been inspiring.

Love Jarrod.

Lee Jarrod Evans

hi again...i thought id relate an interesting experience. i recently acquired one of xanders cd's from Dee Smith (thanks for everything Dee, and thanks to you for all of the equipment(even though you probably think much of my stuff is too noisy)thanks Xander, i felt weird taking some of your stuff, but Dee assured me that you would want it to be used in a creative way, im sorry that i never gave your music the praise it deserved.....i was just listening to your cd entitled IN THIS MOMENT (AKA NOW) ....the interesting thing is the way in which i heard it...last nite aaron dison hooked up my tape/cd player to my reciever so i could play video games and listen to any music i wanted....i picked up your cd and thought it would be a good time to listen to all of those songs that i have gotten to know so well, and had listened to so many times (usually acting distant, as i do sometimes when confronted with pure emotion)....ok, this philips/magnavox cd/tape player (the same one i was talking about) will not play cd-r's (which is what your cd is recorded on)...sometimes it wont play anything...i decided to try to put it in and play it anyways...AND IT WORKED!

then of course i listened to the cd, now the songs have been made sacred, this always happens when an artist that is just getting started passes away (i.e kurt cobain, etc)....great stuff man, keep up the good work....

i tried to play the cd in this same crazy music player and it would not work, i tried many methods, it wont play in the cd/ tape player---crazy music player.....

do little things like that happen to you guys when you listen to his music?

i, for one, cant listen to it too often....but i was wondering..

with love, jarrod evans

Holly Bowen

This was one of my Mother's favorite poems. She wanted it read at her funeral, but we couldn't find it. With the power of the internet, I found it a few years ago. Reading it gives me comfort. I hope it helps all of you mourning the loss of Xander too.

Do not stand by my grave and weep
by Mary E. Frye

Do not stand at my grave and weep:
I am not there. I do not sleep.

I am a thousand winds that blow.
I am the softly falling snow,
I am the gentle showers of rain,
I am the field of ripening grain.

I am in the morning hush,
I am in the grateful rush
Of beautiful birds in circling flight.
I am the starshine of the night.

I am in the flowers that bloom.
I am in a quiet room.
I am in the birds that sing.
I am in each lovely thing.

So do not stand by my grave and cry.
I am not there.
I did not die.

Fonda Lofton

Wilma, Dee, and Bob: You know how special Xander was. It is not often enough that someone comes along in one's life that is so unique. I believe he was born to bring a smile to everyone he met. His eyes twinkled upon greeting, his music was an extension of himself, and his laughter was contagious. He loved music. He gave to it and gave it back to us, and he brought sunlight in each room that he visited. Class could begin routinely, but when Xander arrived, we all knew it. He always made us laugh and really enjoy ourselves. I remember when he was a senior, he felt so passionate about life and music and the poetry of the text that we were working on that particular rehearsal, that he went into this wonderful tirade of expression spontaneously and simply captivated all of the Camerata Singers that day. When he finished, everyone was quite and then suddenly applauded his passionate teaching of what the composer's intent had been when giving us this powerful tool to communicate with. He so wanted each person in the choir to "get it"!! I loved him. He inspired me so. From the time he was merely 11 and began piano lessons until he graduated and beyond, I knew we had something in this young man. I recognized his composer's heart early because he couldn't wait to hurry up and finish the lesson so he could then play for me "his" music. At 11-can you imagine that!! Some people live much longer and do not leave the mark that Xander left with his music, poetry, and his joy for living in his short 22 years. Blessings to you and all of Xander's family and know that we shall always remember Xander because he made it impossible not to. He was remarkable and selfless and gifted. I am fortunate to have had the privilege of being his teacher and friend.

Justin Huddleston

Xander is and was my best friend, this whole disaster came at a very very bad time. A time when Xander was ready to be free as an adult, someone who is the most brilliant person I've managed to meet in my life... well his life was something many people looked forward to greatly. The death is a tragedy and nearly an insult delivered upon us by reality. The future music and joy that someone as purely unique as Xander brings us all... is sadly stopped short by an unfortunate accident, related to some drunk guy with a truck stopped in the freeway. After something so Completely Horrible I only hope we all survive and live a joyful life. Feeling that it is somehow our responsibility to be happy, fulfill our dreams, and spread the joy in the world that was one of Xander's foremost goals. I will go on to have a wonderful life, I hope we all do, while remembering someone who was by far one of the most precious people to ever exist. With all of my love, and a lot of sadness yet to sink in.

Liam DeLaVega

Xander Smith. Words fail me, but I will try to command them as he deserves at least the attempt. Xander always sent out immense amount of positive energy, of love, in every direction as he pushed forward through his life for which he treated as if it were the grandest adventure. I count myself so lucky to have known him. While this may seem an exaggeration, it is not; Xander is the reason I have faith in the world. It was through he that I learned that there is one thing for which we must have faith· each other. He made me believe that we control how positive this world truly is. I was enlightened through his words and ideas that the best balance any of us could ever have would be to embody the fearless and never ending curiosity of a child, the inspiring and positive ideals of a teenager, and the time-earned wisdom of an adult. It was Xander's belief that the only viable and truly productive reaction to the negative energy and horrible events that occur in our world is to smile larger, love more, and embody that which we want to be reality. It is because of this that his death isn't meaningless to me.

People talk about how their loved one would want this, or would want that. I can say without any doubt in my soul that Xander would want us to celebrate that which was his amazing life, instead of mourn an ending. Xander always knew that we should not mourn an ending because that which he believed is true and we must celebrate the beginning of his legacy. A legacy that will continue in each of us that he touched. It will be in the memory of Xander and in dedication to his beautiful ideals that I will press forward through this adventure that is life with the strength of positivity, the ideals of kindness, and the thought that we are all bound together as one.

I don't know how I'll deal with this loss. I know how I should deal with it. However, it is so very hard to continue on in a world that destroys one of it's few beacons of light. The world is a much dimmer place without Xander. My world is a much darker thing without him. I will struggle now to make up for his light...although I may never live up to it, I think he would want me to try, and thus I shall.
-All my heart and soul, Liam

Ben Shewmaker

I met Xander in 2nd grade, and even at 7 years old, I knew he was unique. Conversations never involved gossip about people, like it often can in school yards. Xander never had time for these conversations. He was much too busy coming up with new 'games' we would play involving wizards, warlocks, and of course, music. If Xander was anything, he was passionate. He never did anything with half his energy. His imagination was incredible, and I have never met a better dreamer in my life. But if there was one thing Xander treasured most in life, it was his relationships. He saw in each and every one of his friends something beautiful, something unique, something worthy and capable of love. He had an uncanny ability to discover and bring out the best in people. Discussing his relationships with other people, he never dwelt on negatives or problems, but focused on those beautiful things he could see in people (even things we sometimes could not see ourselves). And although it is almost unbearable to think of living the rest of my life without Xander, I can still feel his spirit inside, encouraging me to become the incredible person he knew I would become. I'll miss you Xander.

Love always, Ben

CLAY

After two weeks of learning of Xander's passing, I felt compelled to come back and read more of the entry's by those people who were touched by his love of life. Instead tho I found myself reading those entry's in his poetry guestbook. The more I read the more I thought, cried, paused, pondered, laughed, and smiled. I came across a journal entry nearly 2 1/2 years ago. One I had written 45 mins before my last final of the semester at Belmont. I realized how inspired I felt after reading your page just minutes before a huge final. All the sorrow and sadness I felt this past few weeks was wiped away for a moment. Thanks for the Smiles, Thanks for the Laughs, Thanks for the LOVE, and Thanks for the Inspiration. WE MISS YOU

Clay

Keith Salter

The last year that I taught at JHS, I had the pleasure of having Xander in one of my classes.

I recently moved to a different house and ran across a letter that Xander had written me, expressing how much he appreciated the knowledge that I had shared with him and that he would miss me.

What he may not have realized is that he was a blessing to me--a daily reminder of what a young man can become when he has focus and a sense of purpose in his life. I saw in Xander many of the things that I wish I would have been as a young man.

While I mourn his passing, I also know that he is now cradled in the arms of the Savior.

Candace Furniss

"The best way is always through." Robert Frost

And we will make it through this most difficult time with each other's strength. I love you so much, Grandma Smith! I had a dream about Xander Sunday night. It was so real. He was playing his piano in the living room. It was a song I had never ever heard before. I stood by his side weeping because it was so beautiful. When he got up we both began dancing, but his song was still playing without him touching the piano. We danced with every ounce of our energy and passion we had, and all of a sudden he started to dance so fast and with such fury that he just disappeared. In the distance I heard his voice say, "I miss life, but it is necessary for all of you to keep living. What you do matters, and all there is to do is love." When I woke up Monday I could not stop thinking about him. I felt so heavy. I had no energy, and I just kept crying on until Monday night. It is so unbelievable and so new...it's going to take a long time just to accept that this has happened. We must allow ourselves to experience the depths of this pain, however we must not keep ourselves closed to joy...we must still allow joy and light to enter our hearts.
Love, joy, and life, forever and ever and ever.

FOR XANDER
By Candace

Thank you for uprooting me
when I was firmly grounded
stuck in the soil unwillingly

Your hands
Grasped my entrenched being
and threw happily it into the
Alarming space of Consciousness

Awake I became in your presence
You, predictably, preceded me by seconds

You activated in me moments of clarity
Surrounded by the solitude of Perfection
You were the catalyst that coated my motives with
heart
and sealed them off with purity

Although I downplayed and even denied your specialness
Afraid that notions of elitism would corrupt the both
of us
I recollect with exclusive giddiness
The ecstatic energy achieved in our coming together
Our voices traveling faster than logic
and our brains speeding past one another's
Breaking all the laws and regulations
of a society we dreamed to transform

Now I recognize the specialness, the rarity of such an
encounter

. . . and it's more than terrifying to imagine a world
without your presence in it
Yet somehow it is

The tragedy and mystery of it all overwhelms me to
such degrees that I become speechless, motionless, and
just quite enough to hear the wrestling tentacles of
new growth reaching out towards the light that you became.

Candace

GRANDMA

Yesterday I visited your Christmas-decorated grave. I turned the volumn up high on the car stereo and played one of your songs, Thinking of You, for you. The words to that song express my love for you so beautifully.

You are my mind's masterpiece.
You live inside my dreams,
And sometimes I fall asleep
Just to steal a kiss.

I've been thinking, thinking of you.
Thinking about all the things we can do.
All the things we'll learn.
I'll swim across all the rivers
if the bridges have burned.
Xander

I bought an ornament with your name and the dates inscribed on the back and part of a poem entitled Merry Christmas from Heaven on the front.

"I love you all dearly
now don't shed a tear
Cause I'm spending my
Christmas with Jesus this year."
John Mooney

I gave one to your Mom too, and she and I both shed some tears, but it comforts us, even though we miss you so deeply, to know that you are forever with God.

I love you forever, world without end, and know in my deepest heart and soul that we will again spend Christmas together. Until then

Linger,

Grandma

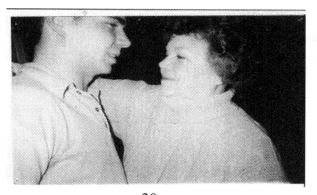

My Precious Xanderiffic Angel, From Grandma

One Year!

Early this morning I visited your grave and left you a single rose. I turned the volume up on the stereo and played "I'm Flying Like an Angel" for you. I love you so much! I miss you!

One Year!

This time last year you were still with us. I was at your house helping the nurse with your Mom when you ran in and asked me to move the nurse's car so you could back your Jeep in and load your equipment for your performance in Memphis.

One Year!

Later that Saturday afternoon I came back to tell you good bye and to ask you to be careful driving to Memphis. You were excited and ready to go. You said "Don't you think I look great, Grandma?" I told you there was a tiny little ink spot on the side of your shirt and you said, "I'll be so marvelous that no one will notice that little spot." You leaned over your Mom's bed and kissed her and said, "I love you, Mom. I love you sooo much!"

One year!

You and I walked together through the living room. We both said our I love yous, I said my be carefuls, and then we embraced and kissed goodbye. My lips were the last to touch that precious face. You got into your Jeep and I, wanting to delay your leaving for just a minute more, opened the front door. You jumped out of your Jeep and said, "What is it, Grandma?" I said, "Knock 'em dead, Baby!" You flashed me that wonderful smile, gave me a happy thumbs up, backed your Jeep out and left on your drive to Memphis--the drive that took you to Paradise.

One year!

At about ten p.m. August 14th, I tried to call you but got your message. I thought you had the phone off because you were performing, not

21

knowing that it, like you, was burned to ashes on the Memphis bridge. I went to bed at 10:15 and prayed for God to keep you safe, not knowing that you had been in His arms for three hours.

One year!

At 4:30 a.m. Mom and Rowdy drove out to let us know about your accident. I actually felt the earth shift on its axis when she spoke the words that ended our life as we had lived it before. Grandpa kept saying, "Oh No! Oh No! Oh No!" Rowdy broke down and had to leave, and in the middle of feeling like my life had ended too, I felt such sorrow for Mom trying so hard to be brave for us. We turned on the Memphis news just at 5 a.m. and the lead story was your accident. In the news report your Jeep was sitting on the bridge burning. Oh My God! Oh my precious Baby!

One year!

It has been hard, and it has been slow, but I have learned to give thanks for all that you left us. I have typed and bound over 500 of your insightful and spiritual poems. You left hundreds of cds of your beautiful voice and gifted piano hands playing your music. We have so many wonderful, movie-star quality, great-looking pictures of you, my gorgeous Xander. You have friends and loved ones who keep in touch with us, and with you through this memorial page, and you left us a lifetime of wonderful memories and so, soooo much love. And you left us your beautiful and sweet Spirit to help us through the hard days and nights of weeping. Thank you, My Love.

One year!

I could write all day and not begin to tell you what you are to me and what your life meant to so many who love you, but I will end this with part of a poem by Emily Dickinson that you loved enough to include in your writings. It speaks of you and who you are.

My candle burns at both ends.
It won't last through the night.
But oh my friends, and oh my foes,
It gives a lovely light.

I will love you forever, world without end.

Robin Carver

Well its been a year and month. I listen to your cd that I bought from your mom last Christmas a bunch, especially last summer. It helped me through a rough spot in my life, one that I still am not complete over, but a vast improvement.

When I listen to that cd its like you right here with me. Your energy and spirit that you poured into its production makes me think "Gosh, its hard to believe he's actually gone."

I wish I would have been able to talk to you, or maybe shared some of your wisdom before you left us. I wish I could start to see what this all means (Your words, not mine). Maybe part of what you left for us here on earth is the wisdom and strength in your songs. I just wish you could have given us a bit more detail. But I guess life is what you truly make of it and its something for us to go out and see what it is for ourselves. Like you used to do.

Well, I think that's all I have to say. Maybe you could become a muse and inspire other artists and reveal to us your secrets. Just a thought.

Amber Stricklin-Miller

Never have I met someone more caring, more outgoing, someone who loved life so much, someone who could light up a room with a laugh. I miss you, Xander. I miss your smile, your laugh, your voice. I walk around campus and expect to see fliers for your next show...and then I realize that there will be no more. Its been a year. A long year. I feel like I should have gone out of my way to get in touch with you. I have all of these regrets about what I should have done when you were here...but its too late. I know that one day I will see you again, and I can apologize face to face... I miss you.

Jenny Pham

My lovely Xander,
Your cd has been in my car since I left. The last thing I told you
was that I love you. I'm so glad. I just now found out that I can't
hear the light in voice again, almost a year too late.
I'm sorry, sweetheart. I'm sorry. I can't explain to you all that my
heart has to say to you.
You changed my life. You saved me and my mom in so many
ways. I have a head and heart so full of gorgeous memories. And
only an "I love you" as our goodbye.
Your car...oh that car! It was crazy driving around with you back
and forth from Memphis. Music CRANKED. The only thing
louder was your voice.
The ball...you looked more fabulous than me that night. And I've
never felt happier.
Lunches, concerts, clubs.
The way your hair was so curly and thick I could barely get my
fingers through it.
And your talent. You were touched by the hand of God. Sitting at
any and all pianos you could get your hands on. And letting
something greater and more beautiful than all of us sing out. I
wanted you to meet my guy. He reminds me so much of you.
So I'll say to you the only way I ever left it with you. I miss you.
"I Love You"

Aunt Donna

I'll never see a 'no swimming' sign without thinking of you Xander.
Even at that young age you knew what you wanted and went for it.
I love you very much, and am so glad you came to the lake over
the 4th so I could tell you how much, it had been way too long
since I had told you . Thank you for giving me that chance. So
goodbye for now sweetheart, but I know it won't be forever.
YEAH SWIMMING SURE.

Erin Smith

It's been so long. It's almost Christmas again. This time I am going back to Jonesboro, so I suppose I will be visiting your grave for the first time since that day. Life is so different now. I spend so much time trying to figure out how to live in this world. Sometimes I still think that I might call you, but then I remember although really I think that I already knew. I think that I will be a writer, but I don't know where this life is going to lead me or where I am going to take it as the case may be. Listen to me. I haven't seen you in so long and all I can do is talk about myself. Forgive me. This season reminds me of you. I remember how you told me about how important it is not to get sucked into the illusions of jadedness-about-the-holidays that so many are prone to fall prey to. You reminded me that although we might not know what we believe, we certainly should appreciate joy in all its forms and what could be more joy-inducing than cold nights, hot drinks, and people you love reminding you of all the reasons why... Oh yes...All for love...in all forms.

I love you, Xander. You have given me a lifetime of inspiration. WWXD (what would Xander do) I think it often and I smile. Your song "Time" runs through my head and I marvel at your insight and try to take your transcendent advice. I love you, Xander. Merry Christmas!

Erin Smith

I thought about you today. I spoke to your mother. Then, a little later I was walking home from the park and a bird flew in front of me and landed on the sidewalk roughly two yards away. As I continued walking this bird would continue to fly into the air a bit and land two yards away from my advancing stride. And then again and again. It might have happened three times or four, but it happened enough to bring me to think of the bird and its spirit and "is this a message from Xander? Is Xander in that bird?" Then a voice came to me that sounded like mine only wiser. It said "Xander is in that bird as he is in all things" The spirit of Xander cannot be confined to a single spirit entity. It saturates all that is. Xander is part and parcel with the world at large, as large as it may be. You, Erin cannot claim to be privy to the secret of what is "really" going on in this crazy world or the truth of spirits or divine entities. However, you can say for sure that the world as you do know it. The world that you experience. The only world that your current ego is ever going to know, is one that is wholly saturated with the spirit of Xander."

As I heard that voice or as I write these words, I feel that I have touched something very central to the nature of being. Thank you Xander.

Today, as I was riding the train to school, I started singing Time. I think I remember all of the words. It made me very sad. I feel funny, like I should write some dazzling, flowery ode to you again, but actually, to tell the truth, I feel sort of drained. I felt those same old feelings wash over me again. I miss you I miss you. I thought about whether or not anyone else will ever know the words to Alladin and Jasmine's A Magic Carpet Ride and sing the duet with me. I wonder if anyone else I meet will delight in singing Belle's theme from Beauty and the Beast. Will there ever again be another person who will confess to knowing all of the Mariah Carey B sides, but poke fun at her trite subject matter in the same breath? I also thought about how I should grab the next person I saw and insist that they listen to me sing Time to them, but I didn't. I had to go to class. I think that I will go to the Rainbow Gathering this summer. I want Candace to see it. I remember when we went together and how magical it was to see you see it. I will speak of you and sing your songs when I am there, as well. I will share the legendary magic of Xander. But I so miss the tangible magic of Xander. Even more, I miss the tangible plain old Xander who had messed-up hair in the morning and worried about his complexion. I love you so much. I don't want to lament here. I want this to be a sacred place of thanks and praise and love. Therefore, I will close this, as I feel those aforementioned lamentations resounding in my head.

You're Sweet, like chocolate, boy
You bring me so much joy
You're sweet like chocolate ohhh
(and other dance anthems we sang)

✷✷✷

HI, Xander. It will be your birthday in only eight days. I remember, because mine in on the 17th too. Maybe I would remember even if it wasn't. I miss you. The other day I was thinking about my interactions with people and I realized that the terms in which I was thinking of them never existed with you. My relationship with you was oftentimes NO-holds-barred brutal honesty for growth or hurt feelings or even a little of both. It was always you that I looked to to reaffirm my sanity. I always figured that even if I was crazy, you were just a little crazier. Therefore, everything would be alright and if you could deal with the world at large then so could I. Well, I deal, but to tell you the truth, things were a lot different for me when you were around to confide in. When everyone leaves the house I sing really loud. And sometimes I wonder why I don't sing so loud when people are around. I guess I am afraid that they would tell me to be quiet. When I think these thoughts I remember that you didn't care about such things. Moments like these make me miss you all over again like you left this life only yesterday. That is all. I will come back on your birthday to say more. So long for now. I love you still.

For Xander
By Erin

I took a shower today As I was getting out I began to think

It was intense and all-at-once

Too meaningful to cry over

This is my life and has been for a while

My memories are all things that have happened and someday I will die

It seems so simple, but I wanted to cry I wanted to cry for profundity

All kinds of predictions are coming true in some way, yet I cannot know

What will happen. The days change and so does my mind

My life isn't what it once was. This isn't a judgment, just a fact

I am getting wiser and more silly and more alone and more social

I was once quasi-hired to inspire the greatest poet I've ever known

He said that I was a Shams to his Rumi, but unlike that legend

He is the one who is gone and I am the one who still searches for him

In everything that is made of molecules

Timothy Burns

When I knew you...back then. I was a different person, full of fury at nothing and anger at everything. I wasn't a good person. I behaved like an ignorant, banal, moron.
I knew you and Erin and Candace. (Sorry I don't know where this is going.)
When I heard about your passing. It left me thinking about my life and my horrid past. About regrets. Regrets are a terrible thing in life, and I don't think you had many of them. My life is plagued by them all, like ghost that haunt me on a hourly basis. You lived free and I envied you for that. I was jealous of your smile. I always thought you were a nice guy, and a good person.I just never told you so. And that's another regret of mine. I wish I could heal a lot of things in my past. It's just hard getting past the scars.
Perhaps all in time, I suppose.

Tim Bowen

I've been dealing with this for a while now by just thinking that you faked this whole thing. I mean, come on, Andy Kaufman faked his own death, Elvis faked his own death, Tupak, so many others, and I think you're in league with them. So why not Xander? I keep thinking that someday soon I'll be somewhere and see you. I keep thinking someday I'll be initiated to some secret Masonic society and you'll be there...

I miss you.

Misti Smith

A year ago tomorrow. It seems like it hasn't been a year, but then again it seems like it has been an eternity. I am not really sure. Maybe it was because I didn't see you alot the last few years because we were both busy with school and other things. I was in Florida on vacation when dad called me to tell me the news. I am leaving for Florida next Saturday. It almost scares me. I am afraid that if I go back to Florida that I will wake up and get a call that something bad has happened. But then again, I trust God, and if it were someone's time to be called home then it wouldn't matter whether I were in Florida or here in Louisiana. I am trying not to let myself get superstitious. Anyways, I just wanted to get on here and let you know that I still think of you probably every day, and I am sure, no, POSITIVE I will for years and years to come. It's so sad how when I had you here to call, I talked to you a few times a year, and now that you are not here, I wish I could call you every day. I let me friends listen to your music all the time. Everyone likes it. Some cry (especially when I start crying). I miss you. I love you.

Misti Smith

I was browsing on the internet this morning before I went to work, and I decided to see if Xander's site was still on here. I am so sorry to hear about Sandi. I didn't know her very well, but what I did know was that she was a wonderful lady and everyone who knew her loved her. I have been thinking about Xander a lot lately because someone I went to high school with was killed by a drunk driver last weekend.

Xander, I still have your pictures on my dashboard, and I still think about you all the time. Your cd still enters my cd player at least once a week. Just wanted to let you know I love you and still think about you. I miss you.

Grandma, Grandpa, and Aunt D, I love you all, too. Dad said something about coming to the lake when school let out. Hope to see you soon. I miss you all, and I love you.

***

I was on my way to teach this morning, and I was listening to my Avril Lavigne CD when a song came on that I don't think I had ever actually listened to the words. This time was different. I have your pictures posted on my dash, and I looked down at you when I heard the words "I wish that I could see you again; I know that I can't." I started to cry, and it hit me that I really am never going to see you again. I guess because we hadn't seen each other very much recently, it didn't seem real or something. It hit me this morning harder than it has hit me thus far, and I just wanted to write and say I love you and I miss you. Here are the complete lyrics to the song. I'm pretty sure Avril wrote this song to her grandfather when he died, and now it's my song to you. I love you.

Na na, na na na, na na
I miss you, miss you so bad
I don't forget you, oh it's so sad

I hope you can hear me
I remember it clearly

The day you slipped away
Was the day I found it won't be the same
Ooooh

Na na la la la na na

I didn't get around to kiss you
Goodbye on the hand
I wish that I could see you again
I know that I can't

Oooooh
I hope you can hear me cause I remember it clearly

The day you slipped away
Was the day I found it won't be the same
Ooooh
I had my wake up
Won't you wake up
I keep asking why
And I can't take it
It wasn't fake
It happened, you passed by

Now your gone, now your gone
There you go, there you go
Somewhere I can't bring you back
Now your gone, now your gone
There you go, there you go,
Somewhere your not coming back

The day you slipped away
Was the day i found it won't be the same noo..
The say you slipped away
Was the day that i found it won't be the same oooh...

Charles Frierson

Dee:
When I look back over 72 years, I am struck by how many of the best and brighest left this world Far before their alloted time. Perhaps we just notice them more because of the lost potential. Your best memorial to him would be to carry on, to do your best to live as he would have wanted it.

My heart goes out to you.

Nicole

You'll be greatly missed by all of us, and I'm sorry that we lost touch after high school. Your music and your poetry will keep your spirit alive for many more years to come. You're awesome Xan! I love and miss you much!!

Xander's mom (Dee)

this memorial to Xander has been such a blessing for me and my family. the wonderful thoughts and memories of Xander are something i will treasure all of my days. as a mother i knew Xander was a remarkable person but i was never really aware of how great he was and how many other people felt Xander's magic and love. thank you to everyone that has written here, this is something i will always treasure and be able to read and read again, as we have printed all the pages. i am so proud of Xander and also of his friends i love each and every one of you. and always know you are welcome here at Xander's earthly home. God be with you all. again thank you from xander's mom, his grandma,his grandpa and Xander. don't think for one minute that he doesn't know all the love you all have in your hearts for him. he will be missed, honor him with spreading love, truth, honesty,kindness, and God bless you all. peace.

Donna Lenners

I sit here this Saturday morning thinking about you, your mom and your grandparents not to mention the numerous friends who are missing you as well. I know your birthday is this Tuesday and I dread Tuesday. I dread this week. I dread this next year as we try to see the man charged with his 4th DWI prosecuted for his offense! I dread the lifetime that all will have without you in it. Now that I have gotten that off my chest I have to look into what I have come to know about you... I rejoice in being introduced to what an inspiring young man you were. I rejoice that I have been blessed to meet your family. I rejoice that you have touched so many lives that people don't live their lives in the same way they used to taking the people they love for granted. I rejoice that I read friends and family are making better decisions due to your needless tragedy. I rejoice in people sitting on tail gates of trucks naming stars after you and finding the brightest one for you. I rejoice that people who haven't gotten to meet you are writing poetery on this site because someone has lead them to this site in your honor and as a love memorial. Xander, although your body is gone your spirit still lives... it lives within each one that thinks of you and carries the xanderisims of you each day of their life. I love Erin though I have never met her, I want to see her dancing and singing at the top of her lungs and living life to the fullest just as you inspired so many of your friends to do! You are truly missed and loved. So much it has been hard for many to think of continuing to live without you. That is the hardest thing is when you love someone so much you can't live without them but you know how much YOU Xander would want everyone to continue living life to the fullest because thats Xander! We Miss you... So many people see your picture through me and my presentations. You XANDER... will never be forgotten and thank you for being with us in spirit to help to carry us through the life we try to live without you.

I can't help to think about you daily...

Juan

Knowing Xander was a pleasure. He was always a bright person, and always made me laugh. Its hard to believe that he's gone. When my mom passed away Xander was there for me, and help me. I always knew i could talk to him. Even though i only met him a couple of times, im blessed that i got the chance. My Prayers go out to his family and friends.

Gary Morris

I taught Xander in my 1st year teaching at Jonesboro High School. He was a very talented musician and great student with a great personality. My prayers and thoughts are with you.

"Music, when soft voices die vibrates in the memory"

God Bless You

Jim

Xander became a friend during his time in Nashville. I never met someone who could light up the room like Xander did, with just a flash of his smile. His music was also inspiring. I would always get excited when I had the chance to talk to him on the phone or exchange computer greetings - casue I always knew he had that smile on his face. My that smile watch over all of us from heaven above, and to the Smith family may God wrap you in his arms and comfort you.

Melissa Allison

I went to high school with Xander and was in the school's production of "Damn Yankees" with him. I played a very minor character and he played Satan. His talent was unmistakable and we were constantly in awe of his ability to take this character that the audience was supposed to hate and make him the favorite character of the show. He dazzled us everyday with his wit and his grace on the stage put us all to shame! He also didn't act like a star. He was just as comfortable sitting in the green room with the chorus people as he was out on stage getting applause and accolades.

I remember thinking very highly of him because I was a sophmore at the time and wasn't a standout performer, so I was quite surprised when he, a star senior, complimented me after a scene we were both in. He had this wonderful ability to make everyone around him feel like they were the most important person in the room.

I ran into to him once after I had graduated, and didn't think he'd remember me after 2 years, but he came right up and hugged me and asked how I was and if I was still in choir. I was astonished because we had never really been close friends, only acquaintances through the plays and through choir.

Xander had a presence that could make the whole room not just light up, but sparkle. You could not be upset if he was around becuase he did his level best to cheer you up, and he was good at it. He was a wonderful person who had the ability to draw the best out of people, and he will be greatly missed.

Sandi Frierson

I cannot begin to express the sense of loss I feel. As a long time friend of Xander's mother, I have known him all my life. I was there when he was born, and have been proud to watch him grow up.

Xander was intelligent, talented, idealistic, passionate, and compassionate.

I will mourn for the baby I held in my arms, for the child who loved to sing along with Dolly Parton, for the teenager I took to his first recording session, and the young man I discussed religion and metaphysics with as an equal.

I never thought such a bright light could be dashed out so easily.

Jerry Bercheen(cousin)

Hmmmm. Kinda hard to know what to say. If only i was more like zander id have the perfect words to say to make everyone smile. Me an zander were more alike than most people i've known. Music, philosophy, and in just all around mind set. Not afraid to stand for your beliefs, despite what the world thought. well i dont know what else to say except, See ya on the other side cuz. Tell grandpa i said hi.

Marc Sexton

Xander touched so many people with his exuberant personality and true love for people. He had an amazing voice and was a natural born performer. He will be truly missed but hopefully his spirit and ideas will live on through his music.

Jim Ellis

Dear Smith family: Our heart goes out to each and every memeber of your family and friends. Xander was a wonderful young man that we all grew to love and respect as a student while at Annie Camp and at JHS. This was certainly a tragic thing and very hard to accept for us all, but please know that each and every one of you are in our prayers at this time and will continue to be for days to come. Please remember that God will comfort you through this and continue to gain strength from that.

Jim Ellis

Annie Camp staff

Brent

I became friends with Xander while he lived in Nashville and had the honor of being his friend for several years. On many occasions I was able to see him bring joy, love, and laughter into the lives of many of his friends. He was an honest, kind,loyal, genuine person who comforted and encouraged me at serveral dark points in my life. I can honestly say that my life is better for him having been a part of it and i will miss him dearly. My heart goes out to his family and all those close to Xander.

Reed & Tim

My deepest sympathy and condolences go out to the family and friends of Xander. Xander was one of those very rare individuals that saw something good in nearly everything. He had an unbelievably warm and kind heart. I'm glad I got to know you Xander. Keep singing ☺

Reed

Paul Bullington

I had the pleasure of meeting xander quite a few times. I enjoyed his style of music, his creativity, his laugh and his smile. he was always so sincere and knew how to make a room glow. i feel a loss today, as do so many others. my heart goes out to his loved ones.

Donna James

I have lots of fond memories of Xander during his Jr. High years. I always enjoyed going with the FBLA to competition at ASU. Xander would always keep everyone in line and encourage them to do their best. He was full of life, energy, and laughter. Even though I haven't seen him in a few years, his grandma would keep me updated on what he was doing. He was truly the light of her life. She just beams when talking about Xander. She is one proud Grandma! May beautiful memories of a life lived to its fullest linger, and the shadow of pain be lessened each passing day. My prayers are with you.

Brenda Brecheen(cousin)

Xander,
The vision I have of you is as a little boy, around 4, squirming to get out of Uncle Bobâs arms when I was trying to take a picture of you all. The feeling I have of you begins in the light I have always seen in Aunt Wilmaâs eyes or heard in her voice when she spoke of you. That feeling continues when I read that so many others also have that light in their eyes and their hearts, only it was a reflection of your light. While it seems that you are gone, you are still here. Your light beams from all those you touched.

To Dee, Aunt Wilma, and Uncle Bob, there are not enough words or flowers or hugs or anything of this earth that can convey the ache I feel for you. Please know that I love you! Remember, you are not alone. This website proves that. Hugs!!! (!)

Uncle Wayne

I am not a man of many words, I only know you were and are loved deeply not only by your family and friends but by the many you have touched with your words and song.We that knew you will always wonder what could or would have been.You will always be with us until we are with you.

(You have gave some means to the meaningless and had a point to having lived)

Scott Schaefer

Xander,

You always appreciated the power I had to express myself in words, but I'm afraid I'm a bit at a loss right now. You were truly a light in my life and in the world. I will always remember the time we spent together. I will always treasure what you taught me and what we shared. Everytime I read Rumi, I think of you and shall always remember you. Foremost, you taught me the power of love. Everytime I go to 80s night and hear "Like A Prayer," I think of you and always shall. You truly were a rara avis, a rare bird. I shall always treasure my time with you; time spent discussing poetry, writing music, and just hanging out. You'll always be a part of me, as well as everyone who knew you.
I don't really no what else to say, so I'll end with a line from Catullus (that Roman poet I'd always quote).

"Atque in perpetuum, frater, ave atque vale."

"And in eternity, brother, hail and farewell."

Michael Moore

Xander,
You saw the inner beauty in me that I never saw a few years back. I know, I am not the only one. I thank you for that. I have a lot of great memories with you. My favorite of course, is just we enjoyed each other's magnificence. How beautiful is that? I like others were afraid of that light that shined in the darkness - but you? Never... Never any regrets. You are a great work of god. I still can feel that magnificence run through my veins. "I want to drive - drive so fast -right into the past the way you rode with me." You are still here with us in your music, writings and those infamous happy spiritual meetings. Keep up the inspirations!
I love you!

Clay (wes)

Xander,
Im gonna miss you man. We havent talked much in the past year but those few years at Belmont here in Nashville you were a great friend and an amazing inspiration to me in the most infinite capacity. You always saw the glass half full and always believed there was hope when all looked hopeless. You'll never know how you touched my life in the few years we knew each other. This very day the CD you made me and titled "Soak up the SUN" sits in my cd changer. There is hardly a time when I bask in the healing ray's of sunshine that I dont think about how you taught me to appreciate the small things in life. Now your shining down your light on this dark world and its our turn to pay it forward and carry your torch you so proudly held. Thank you for teaching me to speak with my heart and not with my mind. Thank you for teaching me to see the ME in me. I'll never forget you. The world is a better place because of you. Your legacy will live in the hearts of all of us you've inspired forever. I'll close with a line from Vince Gill,"Go Rest High On That Mountain".
With all my heart I thank you
Clay (wes) Nashville

Nathan Silsbee

I have known Xander since the 6th grade.When me and him entered into Jr. High me and Xander became very close friends.The reason being is that me and him were in choir together for six years from 7th-12th grade.Now,when I met Xander I thought to myself,this is a kid with lots of enthusiasum and joy in his life.Xander was the type of guy that if you were down and out,he was the one guy that could always cheer you up.I got the honor and privilege to stand and sing in choir with Xander for many years.I will never forget the time when a dance came up,he wore his Coca-Cola disco pants ,LOL!!Xander I think I speak for everyone when I say,that you inspired us all.To all of Xanders family my heart and prayers are with you always.Xander it was a privilege singing with you for 6 years and most of all it was an honor being your friend.I thank God for getting to meet you and being a part of your life.I am going to miss you buddy.Xander,MY GOD BLESS YOU MY FRIEND AND GODS SPEED!!!Jonesboro High School Class Of 2000!!

Holland

This may be stupid, writing to you on a guest book now that you're gone, but I don't care. Why didn't I do it earlier is what I'm asking myself. I haven't talked to you in about 3 years and I am so sad to say that. I want you to know that I thought about you constantly. Your amazingly loud laugh, mastering free cell together in computer class, holding hands in the hall pretending to be a couple, Fiona Apple, our senior prom. You're the only man to ever take me to the prom. I've missed you for three years and I'm going to keep missing you. Thank you for the memories and all the insight and all the laughs. You made me remember to cherish life and to help others remember too. I miss you. Thank you for leaving us your songs.
"C'est tres drole!"

Caroline

I am sorry for the loss of Xander! He will be missed by all! Xander will not be forgotten by anyone who came into contact with him! His extraordinary personality was so strong that he left a lasting mark on everyone he met.

I remember the first day that I met him in Annie Camp Jr. High as we sat near each other in class. We would talk before class began, and to my good fortune, I got to know him better over the years, sharing more classes and working together in group projects. Xander always made the situation better and he could always bring a smile to my face. He admirably could always defend his position on issues. Most of all, Xander's artistic talent was amazing as it only improved over the years, and he will be missed. My thoughts are with you family. Love

Omar Vance

I'm really at a loss for words to describe how I feel. I'd known Xander for about 4 years. It was only in the last year and a half or so that we started spending time together. I was always blown away by his energy and creativity. He was a kind as he was creative and was a good friend to me. I have a habit of trying to hide how I feel about most things but with this loss, I could not. The night I found out I totally brokedown. I spent a long time thinking about the loss but then I remembered the good times we had. We'd talk about Buffy and Angel, guys we knew, he'd play his music, etc. I will have those memories for however long I may live. Xander was very important to me and so many others and I will never forget him. He lives on in this world through his music and the memories of us who were fortunate enough to have known him.

Rebekah

I was just a kid when you were in my brother's junior high class. I remember you winning an award in the science fair, once... not the face, just the name.. You had the craziest sense of humor. I once took an .mp3 from my brother's computer that said, "My name is Xander Smith-ith-ith, and I play the clarinet-et-et..." And though I didn't know you personally, you were the example for us that were just a little... unique, from the rest of the crowd. You showed us how to be "cool" in our own eyes.

Emily Cassandra

Xander was one of my best friends in junior high and high school. One of my best memories ever was our two skits that we performed at exhibition night our senior year, one where I played a Brooklyn waitress at an insane diner and he was an ultra-proper customer that I scolded for being difficult for asking for a table and a chair. Not having that on tape to watch again is one of my biggest regrets. I loved singing with him, talking to him about life and spirituality, and listening to his music. I think everyone at JHS became fans of the Giga-pet song that he wrote during his Giga-pet phase sophomore year. I loved watching him perform, as did everyone. I always loved his poetry. He just had a great spirit that drew people to him, as all of these testimonials show. I'm glad that I was able to see him again several times this past year, because I didn't want to just totally lose touch with him. I'm proud to have known him so well, and sad that more people didn't get to know of him. I will always think fondly of those years in school because of him. My warmest thoughts and deepest sympathies are with you, Mr. and Mrs. Smith and Dee.

Catherine White

Once again a wonderful human being has been struck down by a drunk driver. I know your heart grieves just as mine did when my handsome young 15-year-old son was killed by a drunk driver in 1989. From the photos, it looks like Xander loved life and was a contributor to society. Was he a coach as his shirt implies? I'm so sorry for your loss and wish I could offer more than my understanding. May God bless you and all those who loved Xander. Sincerely, Catherine White, Victim Advocate and past State Chair for MADD-TENNESSEE.

Donna Lenners

Unfortunately I have gotten to read Xander's Poetry and looked at his beautiful photos. I am the Arkansas State Victim Advocate with Mothers against drunk driving and had this horrible tragedy not occurred I would have never seen or known of this beautiful and obviously talented young man. I did cry when I saw yet another promising life cut short by the decision to drink and drive. Dee, I can't imagine what you are going through! My heart breaks for you. To everyone else, I invite you to join in the fight against drunk driving by becoming a member by going to MADD.org. The way that Xander's left this earth is hard enough to handle. To think that the person responsible for this tragedy could do this to another family is unacceptable!

My heart and prayers are with you and your family.

Debra

Dear, Sweet, Xander... I'm very sorry that I never go to know you the way so many have. I remember fondly the times we did share, and thank all of the people responsible for my meeting you. You will remain in my heart, my thoughts, my life for ever. Shine on, talented one, shine on.

Grandpa

My Baby Boy:

Of all my memories of you(and they fill a too-short lifetime) my favorite is when you were about 4 years old and I was taking care of you while Grandma attended night class. One night while we were watching our favorite show (The Boston Pops) I told you each instrument in the entire orchestra while they played. You were like a sponge, absorbing everything Grandpa told you. Grandma came home in the middle of the show and you couldn't wait to show her what you had learned. You had her sit down, and told her each instrument as it was played and you didn't make even a single mistake. She was amazed! I don't know if I helped spark your interest in music, or if you were born with the passion, but I was blessed to be a part of your upbringing. You will always be the ultimate performer in my life.

There are other times I cherish, like the Father's Day that we spent building you a fort. Remember the big bass you caught in the pond, and how I showed you how to hold him by the lip so I could take a picture of you and your catch? I taught you to say your first word, and I remember when the only word you could say was "duck." I was so thrilled that I immediately went out and bought you four live ducks.

This a letter to you, Xander, and to all the people who might read it, to let you and them know how very much you mean to me. My heart will never be whole again.

I love you,

Grandpa

Matthew Sinclair

I've enjoyed "Drive" since my roommate introduced me to it. It helped me overcome the heartbreak of a failed relationship a few years ago...and has become a favorite song since. I was looking forward to becoming a successful artist manager, and trying to get on board for YOUR success Xander...Now, I guess I'll have to wait about 60 more years before I can work with you. My condolences to your family. This is a tragedy which words cannot adequately express. A talent taken from us far before his time...

In Loving Memory,

Matthew Sinclair

Barry

hey lil brother. im sorry for not being around and not being the big brother i should have been. im sorry that i never told you that i loved you, i always wanted t lil brother, then my dad married your mom, my wish fro a lil brother came to pass then i did not treat you like i should have, my sister and i are very sad, i cant tell you in person how much joy you brought me i remember when we used to ply video games on the nintindo and saga games and rememberd who you uesd to tear me up.lol i foundsome thing that you made for me one christmas, many years ago. you had to be 6 or 7 maybe even 8 yrs old i dont remember, how old you were, but i still have it. it sits by my computer. i dont have any pictures of you. but i still have the gift you made. if any one knows xander mom plz tell Dee that i loved xander and i miss him. love your big brother Barry

Mark McBride

I just found out about Xander this morning. as a frind of his in Murfreesboro TN, i was out of the information loop. I had talked to him just a few before this horrible thing happened. I never knew till now. I thought he was just off doing his own thing, and id see him online, or he call, or hed just show up at my door with a hug, and we would hang out all night lie we did.

I am in shock. I cant believe this. I found this site by accident, and im sick to my stomach. his music is playing on my computer right now. he would come over and compose sometimes, and uploaded a bunch to my hardrive. his voice is here right now, its so weird.

im in shock. its been 4 hours sence i found this site. i would call his parents, but i never met them. im so outta his loop, and now even more so. ive thrown up several times this morning. its stiil so weird. he is so alive to me right now. there is no reality of him being gone.

he was talking of visiting me and his friends here in mid-tn last we talked. and now, his promise, his future, his beautiful life will never be lived. he will never be here ever again. god, this is so hard for me.

i dont know really anything, other than what little facts are here. its only been 4 hours. i can still feel his hugs, hear his laugh, i can still see him sad, and socialy nervous. I can still hear him talk about how he loves his familey so very much.

im still in so much shock here. i need other people that knew him, that can explain this to me. its all to unreal.
someone please contact me.

✷✷✷

Sorry that last post, was a little erratic. Im just finding out about this and all. Later I will share memories and whatnot.

This is for his family that I have never met, but heard so much about: I love you guys, and Im so sorry for your loss. Words cannot express. He loved you completely.

And to you space-monkey, my friend, my little guy:
Xander, you know that I loved you. And I know you loved in return. That was never in doubt, or question. And you know that your place in my life, your lessons, your wisdom and wit, will be with me, and all of us forever, till its our time to see you again and beyond.
Your voice is still here, its playing on my computer right now. Your picture looking back at me. And your heart and soul will be forever with us.

Im crying again man, and I know that makes you so awkward. But I am. I miss you so much. Ill live my life missing you, but smiling at the joy you brought the world, and you brought me. You my friend, were the greatest.

Your music will live on. I Promise you.

(from Mark2Xander)

u do not dream tonight
my boy
u sleep

you who are without hatred,
without malice
whose heart is a million
diamonds
whose truth is honest

with a voice,
sounding full and bright
with love

a soul filled with light

flowing ever into
the evermore
a causeway to gods
and legends

for you, because of you
inbetween and ongoing
the promise will be fufilled

that i do not sleep tonight,
my pure friend,
i dream

Xander's Mommy Mom

this is so hard for me. somewhere deep inside i have held on to the belief you would be returning. now to write this means i have to accept the truth that you are now in heaven and one day i will see you again. if the lord would just let me set in the back of the room where i could look upon your beautiful face and hear your sweet sweet music i would be happy. for the first time since you left this world i caught myself singing one of my made up songs(not a xanderiffic song but a mommy one. "i heard the angels singing in perfect harmony and i was mad and i was sad, cause with them i heard you sing. i asked the lord to release from this pain of a world without you. then God spoke to me "first you must learn the words and learn the tune and one day soon you can also sing with the angels in perfect harmony" i am trying so hard but this is the hardest thing i've ever had to face. not an hour or even sometimes a minute goes by that i don't think of you, miss you, love you. if one day it at least becomes bearable that will be answer to one of my many prayers. i know however i will never find the joy in the world that i did with you here and my world is darker now and will never be as bright as you were and are my sonshine. i have surronded my self with things of yours and pictures and poems. its not the same. i walk around this house we lived in for the last 14 years(of course you were sometimes other places) and there is not an inch of this house where your spirit isn't. you are always with me in my heart, although its been broken with your leaving. i talk with you and God and sometimes i feel you holding me telling me its ok you will see me again and that heaven is such a wonderful place there are no words to describe it. i know i must go on at times (most of the time) its just so hard, i feel as though i'm walking in water chest deep. i'm sorry i'm not the wordsmith you are. maybe there just aren't the words for me to express how much i love you and how i miss you so much. you were my son,my friend,my confidont(as you know i'm not a good speller and don't have your talnets in expressing my thoughts. but you always understood and loved me in spite of my many shortcomings. my hands are shaking so much this is so hard please help me lord. its saturday night and these are hard nights as thats when the lord called you home at 7:15, i'm conviced that you were a messenger,an angel that was sent to spread messages of love, honesty you had a mantra you would say that was some thing like this "be kind, be true, be honset and love better",and when God felt you had spread that message enough to others so they could then spread the message he called you home to rest and find the true peace that this world does not offer.i will try to honor you with your words and messages until it is time for me to leave this earth and look upon your beautiful face again. i wrote you song when you were a baby it was written on one of the patches of your memory quilt i made for you.(you never wanted to put it on your bed as you were afraid it would get messed up,and i often wondered about the two years it took to make it, now i know it was to wrap you in the mother love of having sewn by hand,something to place your earthly body in to its final resting place. but that is just a shell and now i know you are flyin like an angel. my beautiful,beautiful,beautiful boy, who was becoming such a wonderful man. i am so proud of you and in awe of what a great person you were. you are truely my hero. the words to the lullaby i wrote were "xander pie don't you cry mommas goin to sing you a lullaby, sad and sweet tickle your feet momma she fix you good things to eat. xandercon you're so funny you think the world is milk and honey, thats ok anyway momma she play with you today." i love you more than i could ever write the words for,and i miss you so much my world is so empty and my heart has an empty place and sometimes i feel its broken into so many parts of you, but its still there with love and so many good memories. thank you for leaving me so many memories, and your music and poetry and love. as i said on each occsion you would leave to good spread your xander magic and my last words to you "be careful, you carry my heart with you." again i am so proud of you and have been blessed to have you in my life 22 years, of course you hear this as i write it, you were never mine, you belonged to the world and all good things in it. God blessed me with having you as part of my life you were loved and wanted from the first minute of conception,i think you knew that i hope you did. its to hard to say good bye but i will say until we see each other again,i love you so much,forever and forever your mommy mom.

Genny

i've still had a hard time with this, from what i remeber from you is you were always happy and had the biggest smile on you face. love and peace is what you were about. i remeber a time i guess you were about 8 years old and we were throwing away an old bed. the frame of it looked like a stage, (well big enough to hold about 3 8 year old kids
and you were playing on the little red keyboard you had and ben was playing on your bongos and there was another kid but i cant remeber who he was. but anyway you always loved music. and as i look at the picture of you i have on my wall, i still see the same look, you always loved people and people loved you. i know anything we say to the lord about you, you can hear. you will be missed by all. i see the man you had become, and i'm so proud of you. i do love you dearly and i'm sorry i never told you. and i have a few other xander moments that i'll always keep with me. god bless you, peace and love, that was what you were about. i'll see you later little brother. keep the faith, genny

ONE MORE THOUGHT, I REMBER THE SLUMBER PARTYS WE HAD HAD GROWING UP. YOU HAD YOUR FRIENDS OVER, I HAD HAD MINE. WE'D WAIT FOR THE LIGHTS TO GO OUT UNDER THE DOOR, LOOKED AT ONE ANOTHER IN OUR BEST MISCHIVIOS SMILES, AND IT WAS ON. ALL OF US HAD FUN, THROWING PAPER BALLS AND PIZZA CRUST TRYING TO GET IT ALL CLEANED UP BEFORE THE PARENTS WOKE UP. THOSE AND MANY MORE I'LL KEEP WITH ME. GOD BLESS YOU XANDER, MAY YOUR MEMORY KEEP US ALL WARM WHEN WE ARE MISSING YOU. MAY THE LOVE YOU HAVE GIVEN US ALL LIVE ON. WE WILL MISS YOU. LOVE ALWAYS, YOUR SISSY, GEN

Mark

Hey Xander

I havent written in a while to you, as this is still very hard for me. I try to be brave, strong and wise, have courage for others, and help them see light, where there is dark.
And I try to do this for myself.

But I miss you so much. I still get mad everyday, that you are not with us. I am very angry, and still break down. I had one of these moments the other day at work, and I felt so trapped, and isolated. I was overcome with the feeling of injustice of your demise, and of the fact that you deserved so very much more. If I could trade places with you, buddy, I would right now. You deserved a full span.

But, thats is survivor's guilt, and I know that.
I just wanted so much for you. And you deserved so much.

And, its werid, you not being here. My mind still holds out, that this is a misunderstanding somehow. I know the truth, but my spirit still cannot embrace the reality of your death.

Erin was talking about Buffy season 7, and that brings me back to when Kevin and I, got you into Buffy... and it was right at the start of season 7. That mememory of you here in the living room, still makes me smile... you asking who all the characters were, and their stories.

I remember letting you borrow my Angel season 1 boxset, just before you moved. (and you taking it with you)
And I remember all those times, you would call up, feeling guilty that you still had it, and promising to return it.
I never corrected you, becasue listening to you get so worked up about it, was, well, very sweet.
And I was just waiting on the day, that you would give it back.... for me to put both your hands on it, smile, and tell you that you can keep it. It was going to be a little supprise for you. And now, I cant.

I so miss you man. You NEED to be here.
And in your abscence, as always, I will keep the faith, keep
fighting the fight, and always try, to see the light in the dark, and
help others. Just the same thing I would do, if you were here
now.....

I dont have any answeres Xander.

All I have is questions.
And the quiet stillness, that comes from your memories, as well as
the outrage that you are not here.

Sorry bud. Its how I feel.
And you would want me to be honest always. Never delude
myself.
And, Im going to feel this way, perhaps for the rest of my life,
untill its my time as well.

Hopefully, I can see your gave soon. Its important to me.
Maybey I can get away from here, somewhere around X-Mas time,
when work is shut down.
No promises though.

Love you, and miss you.
Like always.

-Mark

Jaye

Xander,

I'm so sorry to hear that we have lost someone so special you had a gift from heaven. You had the heart of gold like the best. I will always miss the talks and the late night chats we had my dear friend. You will for ever and always will have a place in my heart. You are the main reason why I still am alive.if it wasn't for you I wouldn't be still hear today, B.c you looked out for the night that I had my car crash and you helped me get better, an see the better day of tomorrow. If I took anything from you I can say that I learn the most preciouse advise from someone so dear. Now you are where only angel are amoung us. Please tell My luv teague That I haven't forgotten him, So now I have 2 garden angels looking over me. Thank you Xander (xoxoxo) For touching mylife....(* Friendship *)Somewhere tonite we come alive,Two hearts ignite we're one of a kind.Here we are undivided by anything Just you and i,We've come so far no one else could everSteal away what we confide...Who wants to know? We stick together we're never apart,Everybody knows who we are.Because we are one we do it .We come together and stronger we are

Just when the world can tear us apart,We go on as one we do it in unison.Gleam of an eye, flash of a smile,Never too shy playin' ever so wild.Here we are i', relying on no one else.But you and i we've come so far No on else could ever steal away what we..Confide who wants to know?Here we are undivided by anything.Just our friendship.We've come so far no one else could ever...Steal away what we confide in each other...

Grandma

My Darling,

You must have been there with open arms this morning to welcome Sandi to paradise. I can imagine your deep conversations about life, love, metaphysics and all things beautiful, spiritual and thoughtful. Of course, you both know the answers to all your questions now. Ms. Lofton said to me when you left us, "I have found comfort in thinking that We have everything to lose with Xander gone, but Xander has everything to gain." It is that way with Sandi, she had everything to gain, and you gained a reunion with one you have loved all your life.

I don't know what will happen with your web site now that Sandi is gone, but while it is up I want to post a poem that you sent to me, and also part of my response to it. You wrote the poem back in March of 2002, and like so much of what you wrote and said, it seems that you knew your time here was short. The poem is:

DRAGONFLY HEART

I wonder how I'll ever find the answers
When I don't know which questions to ask?

I wonder how I'll escape the web of you,
When I still have miles to go, and so much to do?

I wonder where do I go from here,
If I can't go there with you?

How will I ever explain, and make clear
This sad blue-green sea in me I've seen?

How can I know that you know what I mean?

I will stand on the edge of the land
And let the sun on my face speak for me.

I'll cover my soul with diamond-dust sand,
And wash away, unnoticed with the tide.

Until someday, someone
Will find the message of me
In a bottle
On some distant shore.

Xander

I was touched, and a bit concerned when I read your poem, and
wrote back:

"Hi Precious,

Am I reading more into your poem than you intended to say?
Probably am, but you are such a heart string to me that I sometimes
do that.

Anyway, the message of you will not only be found on a distant
shore. The messsage of you is right here, right now, this moment in
time. You are the message! The message will survive forever in
your music and words, and many are those on distant and near
shores who will be touched by your insight and cheered by your
joy in life. You have been given the tools to make a difference in
this world and to touch lives of those who love you deeply (like
me) and those who only know you through your written words.
The blue green sea in you is not easily explained because it is a
restless expectancy that gives you the sensation of endless.

Endless is motivational, makes you want to write, play piano,
compose, sing, dance, study, run with the wind, explore your
feelings and imagine all the possiblities with some sort of wonder.
It makes you stand in awesome reverence and joyful exuberance. It
is the catch in your breath when you look upon the ocean, or
experience the breath of freedom that comes on a sunny day when
you stand on the edge of the land with the sun on your face. It is
the feeling you experienced when you wrote poetry to the great
tree as you caressed its bark with your piano-soft hands. . . . I am

probably putting too much significance into a beautiful and touching poem that was written in a pensive moment, but concern is Grandma's job. 😊

Now to a lighter subject, two more days until Easter Break! Can't wait to see you. I love you too much!!!

Linger,

Grandma"

Oh my Darling! I still love you too much, and must remind myself daily that "you had everything to gain." I just ache with missing you, and I guess I always will until I, too, am reunited with you in eternity. I love you.

Linger,

Grandma

p.s. Give Sandi my love.

Annie

Hi my name is annie i dont know who Xander is but Mrs.Donna came to my school today(vilonia jr. high) and showed us the pasting of her daughter on a slide show and told the class it would be nice to view this website so i am! its a very beautiful site and i think its great to have this so people can express there feelings about Xander i just wanted to say that my prayers and love is with Xanders family and Thanks Mrs.Donna you made a differnce today in class i was NEVER planning on drinking and driving becuase i have also lost a friend VERY CLOSE TO MY HEART but it just amazed me how you could do this as a job thank you so much! You are great and i look up to....and i am in the FADD...Friends Aginst Durnk Driven!! God Bless Everyone!
Annie
Age:13

mommy mom

xander i'm sure you have found sandi by know it comfortes me to know that you and she are having those intelligental converstions ou both loved so much. she loves you so much and was with me from day one of my pregency of you and she like i fell so in love with you from the start. love her as i know you do. with all my love to you. i miss you more and more every day. and its suppose to get easier but i find it gets harder, i keep thinking somewhere in my mind that you will come home, but the realizion of the hard to accept truth is you are at home. i miss you , my friend, my sonshine, my sppirit and soul. you are always with me amd i know i cry tears, selfish tears, in the knowlege of you being some where so wonderful that is is beyound comprehension, at least mine and its not mine to know until it is my time, i no longer fear death as it will bring you closer to me. i love you more than any words can express only GOD KNOWSHOW much love i have you and for sandi and for
god. i miss you i love you, i love you so muchyour mother who was luckey enough to have you be a part of my worldl,and you will always be....love for ever xander-con...mommy mom

60

Ben

Xander,
Please forgive my lack of communication. It's not that I haven't been thinking of you for the last several months. It has been absolutely the opposite. My mind never seeems to wander very far without stopping on some memory of you each day, really. Only, right after your death, I was starting a new teaching job, and perhaps as a result of the pure shock and denial I was feeling I threw myself into my new job and tried to force you out of my mind. But you don't just love Xander for 14 years and go about your life as if nothing much had happened. Perhaps now as some of the shock has abated, my heart is being allowed to grieve at last, and you seem more in the forefront of my thoughts than ever before. My mind still hopelessly tries to wrap itself around the whole situation and try to answer those questions which are never fully answered. I miss you. I really, really miss you. It always seemed that at times when things seemed hopeless, or so full of painful emotions, that you could console and comfort with an almost unhuman ability. It hurts that the one person who could bring you out of despair like no other is the one who is gone. And so instead I linger on your music, your poetry, and memories of your smile, your optimism and your love. It helps somewhat, but the pain, I think, will only diminish with time.

All my love,

Ben

Andrew Linnell, L'Wara, Afghanstan

Xander,

It's hard to believe that you are gone now. You were a beacon of light in so many people's lives. I am happy that I got a chance to know you again before I left Jonesboro.

Krystle

Xander,

I'm finally getting around to writing in here....

The few memories i had with you, now run through my mind every single day. Especially, the time at the lake when you TERRIFIED me with that crazy bear story! I wish there were more memories. Every time i think of you I always imagine you preparing to dive off the top of castle rock! You were always the brave one! .... Though I am unable to recall as many times together as others, you still inspire me! Through your music, your poetry, your determination, and your love. I have learned from you. I have learned that faith is constantly growing, if you allow it to. And that time is very valuable, every second of your day should be applied towards something. Most of all Xander, what you have done for me. Is given me a reason. A reason to make good decisions, a reason to discover my talent, a reason to accept, a reason to love, but most of all.... a reason to live! A good friend once told me ... "You have to live, for those who can't!"

I still talk to you every day, Xander! My best friend loves your music as well. One night after work i was listening to it (which i do nearly every day) and he was curious as to what it was and i told him. That night we sat out on the tailgate and found the brightest star in the sky and named it after you. Sometimes he'll call on a cloudy night looking for the star and i always tell him... look for the only one shining!

You really were many peoples shining star. Now you will forever be mine! I LOVE YOU AND MISS YOU SOOOOOOOO SOOO MUCH!

Grandma and Grandpa!-

I LOVE YOU SO MUCH! I really wish we could spend so much more time together. Hopefully we will make it down to the lake this summer! That would be great. I miss you!!!

mommy mom

how i miss you. every molecule of my being changed that distane yellow yesterday when you weren't so far away. now i understand so many of the lessons you were tring so hard to teach me. those life lessons, heart sounds, feelings deeper than one can feel. what perfection you are. of course as the mommy mom i always thought you were 'all that and a bag of chips', i just did'nt realize the extent of your influence, the deepth of your knowlege, the magnatude of your love. how i miss you, more every day, its harder now than it was a year ago. i guess for the past 14 months i felt i could fix it, figure out how to get you home, help you save you, find that path to heaven and bring you back. i know that is all irrational but as when people try with good intentions try to tell me, you are forever young, perfect and flyin like an angel, doing things, being, what we on earth can not comprehend. as we shouldn't be able to, thats what makes the spirtual afterlife such a mircle, the not knowing. i know rational. but emotion rules my spirit, my soul, my longing for you. and emotion is anything and everything but rational. i love you. that hollow hurting i feel constationly, is not something i want to 'get over'. why would i want to get over you. i allow my grief to be, to remember, to love you constantly. i've been reading rumi, and have been seeing why your "kindred heart" friends said you were the rumi to their shams. you are forever, your music, your words, i hope to be able to compile and share with the world as i know you had knowledge and the ability to share it beyond my comprehension. the world could benifit so much hearing, reading your wise words. xanderisms. as i read one book you left me about rumi, i started writting free verse about you and how i could try to help others know you and hear your words. i wrote the first poem i've written since that summer of 2000 when you left for nashvagas,belmont. as at that time i thought my heart was breaking, how ignornat i was, i am. there is no way to explain this pain, and you hope, pray, that no one should ever have to. oh, sometimes i fall asleep just to steal a kiss. my poem, my message, my thought for my love. never will i be the same, my world is colder, darker, and so much more lonely. we loved each other uncontionally, you thought i was pretty, you believed in me, and i always in you. my friend, my teacher, my love, my son, never will i know that kind of love again. someday, we will met and talk and hug and laugh and love without our voices making a sound, heart sounds only and that will be enough, how i miss you.

MISSING YOU
you are sitting next to me
who, what, when, where,
you became.
you come to me, you comfort me.
more than one should ever have to understand.
do not ask 'why' or 'how'.
we do not want this magic to disappear.
just accept this gift God gives us.
God's endless love.
for you,
for me,
for we.
the image, the smell, the feel, of you to me.
i ache, i miss,
the hand of God comforts me, my heart is full.
i love better,wiser,fuller, more than i could ever explain
i am in god.
god is in me.
you are now a part of God in a way no mortal could understand, no
i don't truely understand, i just 'know' i accept.
no going back.
no moveing toward
you are
i am
we are love
i am in God
God is in me.
you are Gods hand.
He allows it to be,
as only love can do.
God is love,
Love is Godly.
you are

i am
we.
all three are love
and all are complete.

loving you forever, mommy mom

forgive my grammer, my spelling, my feeble attempt to commicate
my wanting to illuminate as this humble student beings to try to
understand, really understand the teacher,
the master wordsmith. nothing will ever hurt me as this loss has,
this pain, ache, longing, amazes me daily, that i do not die. you
would think that to feel this pain so intensely to toe the line
between insanity and reality, to know i move just one inch and i
would dissappear. but i maintain. i keep walking in this sand, with
water chest deep. as i believe i will see you again, be with the Lord
and hear you sing in God's heavenly band. to not believe, what
madness that would be, as then it would all be for not.
no, i believe, i love, i wait to kiss that smiling beautiful face and
hear that voice that will calm me. look upon the beauty of the Lord
and be at peace. until that time i pray, i wait, i love and miss you.
forever your mommy mom.

Devon M. Scott

It's amazing how time moves after someone so special crosses
over. It seems like just the other day I was scratching my head
trying to figure out how a year had passed. Of course, I have cd's
in the car & music on my computer, and a picture on my shelf.
Since we were already separated by distance and hectic schedules,
I guess it's easier to feel like I'm simply waiting for the next time
we get to visit. In a way, I suppose I am. But that doesn't mean I'm
not missing the Xander madness.

side note: Dee - I've misplaced your number & address. Please
send to me via e-mail or call. DMS

doesnot comb hair (Preston)

i wish you would have still been around
by the time i came around.
i think we would have gotten along together
and had some good times.
and you were a fellow musician.
and also i think you would have been
a good friend in gil's half of the family.
i like your cousin alex bridges a lot.
i think we talk about you some
when he comes to visit misti and i.

i think "in this moment" could be like
paul mccartney's "chaos and creation in the backyard"
had been dreamt up and written by elton john.
you're a...genius.
i never got to meet you, so
the hole reserved for you never got filled.
love & peace

xanderifficsmom

I LOVE YOU SO MUCH, MISS YOU MORE EACH MOMENT,
AND ACHE SO AT THE THOUGHT OF NOT SEEING YOUR
BEAUTIFUL FACE,NOT BEING ABLE TO TOUCH,TO KISS,
TO TALK WITH YOU. MISSING YOUR INFORMATION MY
TEACHER. YOU ARE MY SALVATION, MY HOPES FOR
HEAVEN, AND FOUND KNOWLEDGE THAT ONE DAY,
WHEN THE LORD IS READY I WILL SEE YOUR FACE-IN
THE WAY THAT THE LORD PERMITS-AND KISS YOU
HEAVENLY. YOU ARE MY HEART AND SOUL. ALWAYS
YOUR MOMMYMOM

Elissa Douglas

I am Xander's cousin. I knew him in a different way than most people who have left their thoughts here. When he was a small child I knew him from seeing him at family get togethers with Aunt Wilma and Uncle Bob. I loved it when Xander was there; he was 12 years younger than me and I adored playing with him! (I was the youngest grandchild and it was great having someone younger than me to play with for a change.)

Later when I moved to Arkansas, I knew him from the lake. I spent lots of time swimming with him. I will always remember Xander standing on top of Castle Rock reaching out as though he could touch the sky.

I regret not knowing the side of Xander that everyone talks about here. I feel a real since of loss that I did not get the opportunity to know that side of Xander. I loved Xander very much.

I love you Aunt Wilma and Uncle Bob,

Timothy Bowen

Hey buddy. It's been a while since I've wrote to you, but that doesn't mean I'm not thinking of you. I published all the poetry you had online in a book called "Never Forget Me," and am now getting this book set for print. I'm also getting some more of your poetry published, next one's gonna be called "Love's Confusing Joy." As I sit here at my desk typing your poetry, and compiling these letters from loved ones to you, I can almost feel your spirit smiling down on me.

I know I should probably visit Dee more often, but life comes at you fast, and I'm sure you understand. I still love you brother, and still cry sometimes when reading your poems, hell, sometimes when typing them out.

But I feel that this is a labor of love, and it's giving me some experience. I've got a few more publishing projects going on, and hope to get into more. I finally found something that I love to do, and think I'm somewhat good at, that might make me a living.

There's way too many people up there for me to ask you to say hi to, but if you happen to bump into Rumi or Hafiz or William Blake, give 'em a raspberry and tell them Tim said you're a better poet then they are!

FOREVER YOUNG

I'm still young,
and somehow I'll always be.
There's a little part of me
that is forever free.
The wind moves over the sea,
through the trees,
and through me.
And night falls over my
shoulders
like a costume,
as I begin
to play out my dreams
under the stars.

Xander

In Loving Memory of
XANDER SMITH
May 17, 1982 - August 14, 2004

Happy Birthday, Love.
Mom, Grandma and Grandpa

Jonesboro High School
Jr.-Sr. Prom, April 17, 1999

YOU LEFT TOO SOON

I can't forget the simplest things,
Expressions on your face.
Like where there once was a fullness in me,
Now there's just an empty space.
So many memories.
So many mornings.
So many lonely, lonely, lonely afternoons.
We could have shared,
Had you been there,
But you left too soon.
Xander

In Loving Memory of
XANDER SMITH
May 17, 1982 - August 14, 2004

*Although, Love, we are heartbroken that you are
no longer with us, we find comfort in knowing
that you are forever with God.
We love you and miss you.*

*Mom, Grandma
and Grandpa*

©Jonesboro Sun

Special thanks to Denetrice Smith (RIP), otherwise known as Xander's mom, for providing pictures, and well, Xander himself!!